T0078434

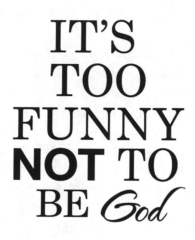

IT'S TOO FUNNY **NOT** TO BE *God*

More From Brenda F. Ferguson

Services:
- Consultation Organization Alignment
- Ministry Training and Development in the areas of
  - o New Members Programs
  - o Prayer Teams
  - o Altar Workers
  - o Pastoral Care (members)

Founder and CEO of Creating Flow, Inc.
- Inspirational speaker, available for conferences, work- shops, and special services

For booking information, contact:

Brenda F. Ferguson

www.indeedflow.com

Brenda@indeedflow.com

469-755-3805

Creating Flow, Inc. P.O. Box 2202

Grapevine, TX 76099

ALIGNING FOR SUCCESS!

BRENDA F. FERGUSON

IT'S TOO FUNNY NOT TO BE *God*

REVISED EDITION

authorHOUSE®

AuthorHouse™
1663 Liberty Drive
Bloomington, IN 47403
www.authorhouse.com
Phone: 833-262-8899

Published by AuthorHouse 12/17/2020

ISBN: 978-1-6655-1125-4 (sc)
ISBN: 978-1-6655-1124-7 (e)

Library of Congress Control Number: 2020925143

To those who mean more to me than I have words to describe—
Elder Simon J. Norwood, Jr. (father, deceased)
Bernice R. Norwood-Willis (mother, deceased)
Bishop Gary Hunt and Lady Ethel M. Hunt (godparents, deceased)
Gerline Hatter (sister)

My grandchildren:

Hannah E. Ferguson
Evan A. Ferguson
Mya G. Ferguson
Alinah N. Ferguson
Jaxson A. Ferguson
Miloh A. Mitchell
Judah A. Ferguson

He will yet fill your mouth with laughter and your lips with shouts of joy.

—Job 8:21 TLB

CONTENTS

FOREWORD

Experiencing the prophetic can be like undergoing surgery. At times, it can be so intense in the way it affects the lives of people, that every now and then God has to raise up an anesthetist. My mom is the anesthetist. You do know who that person is, right? That's the person who numbs the patient from the pain of an operation they must undergo.

I've never known a person, or had a friend, that did not enjoy my mom's company. She's not just a people-person, but she's anointed for people.

Because of this, I've seen her deliver precise and strong prophetic word to individuals in ways that cause them to let their guard down and hear a word from the Lord that they may have rejected from someone else.

I believe this book carries the spirit of that reality. There are times in our lives where the things God is allowing to process us and mature us can seem hard to bear.

It is in such times that we need a reminder of the up side of things. Even to the extreme of when God is correcting us, the scriptures teach that he does so only because he loves us.

God wants us to see things from his perspective. He wants us to know there's always hope even in our darkest moments and that there's always joy even in the midst of sorrows. Consider this book an anesthesia to help you get through the operations that God may be allowing in your life to process you into a deeper relationship with himself.

Apostle Jonathan Ferguson
Ferguson Global

ACKNOWLEDGMENTS

"Yes indeed, it won't be long now." God's Decree. "Things are going to happen so fast your head will swim one thing fast on the heels of the other. You won't be able to keep up. Everything will be happening at once—and everywhere you look, blessings! ..."

—Amos 9:13–15 MSG

I am so grateful to God for speaking this word into my life in February 2016. This word along with other prophetic and rhema words, gave me a supernatural hope and strength to move forward. This book and many other blessings are just the beginning, so first I say, "Thank you, Jesus!" There is one word I use of- ten, one way or another—relationships. I could write about that subject, both the good and the bad.

Truly, God has blessed me with strong, healthy, awesome, and pure relationships that have been the 'wind' behind me pushing me through tests, trials, traps, difficulties, disappointments, and discouragements; while pushing me right into my purpose, passion, and God-given design. Each of them has played strategic, crucial, and integral parts in my life. I count myself truly blessed because God has graced me with the ability to say, "Thank you," and show my appreciation to my family, friends, Pastor Dwayne Hunt and Lady Di, the Abundant Grace church family, other ministry families, spiritual sons and daughters, godchildren and godparents, and the intercessors that God assigned to me. They know that we are all 'fitly joined together every joint supplying the other.' There is no mistake about it, I believe they are smiling and saying, "She is talking about me"—and I am. As I'm thankful for everyone who has influenced my life, there are a few I have pulled on almost daily in my process of writing. Allow me to publically thank my only sister, Gerline Hatter (Memphis), Lady Fran-Cuz (Michigan), Greta J.-Cuz (Memphis), Phillip G.-Cuz (Memphis), Anetria W. (Michigan), Micheale B. (Memphis), Bettie M. (Memphis), Paris D. (Memphis), Latasha S. (Wisconsin), Diane G. (Memphis), Diane N. (Memphis), Lisa W. (Memphis), and Dr. Alma H. (Memphis). Each one, without hesitation, has brought to the table the much-needed unconditional love, prayers, patience, skills, corrections, rebukes, valuable advice, and much more.

Last, but not least, this mother will never forget her children—David, Jonathan, Rachel, and Elizabeth. Three have married, adding to my life two amazing daughters-in-love, one son-in-love, three granddaughters, and four grandsons. I have dedicated this book to my grands, my 'seven heartbeats.'

I thank my four children. Their love, calls, support, and encouragement have made and continue to make my heart sing. Thank you for being your unique you. You never gave up on me. I value each of your individual gifts in my life. I tell the world that I'm glad we are family.

INTRODUCTION

It's funny to me how much time is spent on capitalizing on the bad, the negative, or the works of the flesh. If we're not doing it now, we have done it, I know I have. After going through one test or trial after the other, knowing that God alone is my help, I began to take time to see how well I really knew God, his attributes, and his character after all of these years of serving him. It's the same in a relationship, if you don't know the person, their strengths, their character, etc., you may miss the benefits that come with who they really are in your life. Daily I want to know Jesus more, especially the power of his resurrection. I plan to be a partaker of all that comes with his death, burial, and resurrection. Just thinking about my Lord dying for me ignites a love that I can't ex- plain, but I am very grateful. Jesus didn't stay dead when he died. He got up. When he left, he did not leave us powerless; he made it possible for us to receive the Holy Spirit to live inside us so we can bear his fruit.

We often quote Galatians 5:22–23 KJV (But the fruit of the Spirit is love, joy, peace, longsuffering, gentleness, goodness, faith, meekness, temperance: against such there is no law.) in many of our Sunday School lessons at one point or another. I find the written or- der very interesting. I want to go deep. What if this fruit is listed in priority? What if the list carries the same weight as when we read a genealogy? My thoughts are that we should be more aware of how crucial it is to bear good fruit intentionally and purposely. If the fruit of the spirit is in an order, and we get the first one (love) right, then there will be more joy, peace, and so on. I am so glad God added joy.

How does joy look or sound? I have been told and believe it is laughter. The feeling of joy brings laughter. It is the best medicine and God showed us how to do it, he laughed at our enemy.

It is time for us to stop overlooking what can keep us healthy, peaceful, young, contagious (in a good way), all but pain free; well, read the book and I'll tell you more—laughing. Jesus said in John 15:11 KJV, "These things have I spoken unto you, that my joy might remain in you, and that your joy might be full." I would think laughter would be manifested too. As you continue this conversation by reading this book, I invite to you visit a current situation in your life, even though it may be painful and ask for a 'fresh' revelation of Nehemiah 8:10 " ... for the joy of the LORD is your strength."

Listen, if you think I am writing a book of jokes or that this book is a joke, you are wrong. I pray that you gain a creative perspective of seeing some of the strange and unique ways the Lord would have you do things, even if it seems absolutely crazy. It's just like in the Bible days—walking around a wall quietly for seven days without talking, an axe head floating on the top of the water, a talking donkey, a donkey seeing an angel then sitting in the middle of the road and lastly, the Lord saying that the army is going to be weeded out by the ones (obedience) who will "lap like a dog'. I could go on and on. I love it!

God is saying, "be willing and obedient" no matter how weird it seems. I have numerous testimonies where it didn't make sense, but I obeyed; and not only did he bring me out, he did it with joy and laugh- ter. It's not recorded, but I can only imagine the joy and laughter in the Bible days at their fellowships, when they spoke of their victories after obeying what seemed 'funny.' How could it not be God? Yes, I've had many sleepless nights of tears and anguish, but then I learned in 1 Corinthians 1:25 KJV that "the foolishness of God is wiser than men; and the weakness of God is stronger than men." To know and to see him where others may not have looked has been too funny not to be God.

So enjoy your reading as I (and others) share stories of how God has brought us out with joy through reading and writing.

CHAPTER ONE

LAUGHTER AND JOY FOR THE SOUL

Proverbs 17:22 KJV states, "A merry heart doeth good like a medicine ..." Many times I have wondered how important it is to explore that verse and find every way possible to apply it. When I take a look at all the sick- ness in the world, it causes me to pray and look for solutions. There is sickness in our minds (emotional), in our bodies (physical), and yes, in our spirit (spiritual).

God's desire is to live inside us. It is for us to invite him to come fill us and live inside us. We should allow him to be that power we need dwelling inside us daily. In 1 John 4:13 KJV it is put this way, "Hereby know we that we dwell in him, and he in us, because he hath given us of his Spirit." We are God's children and because he actually lives inside us, we have his DNA, his characteristics. My prayer for you as you read this book is found in Romans 15:13 KJV—"Now the God of hope fill you with all joy and peace in believing, that ye may abound in hope, through the power of the Holy Ghost."

God is the God of laughter. He created man in his own image. Daily, we should seek to be like him in every way. We become more and more like him daily, as we abide in his presence. Since God is a God of laughter, how can we be less than a people of laughter. From the very beginning, he knew the benefit of laughter and joy in our lives. In fact, speaking of the beginning, let's go all the way back to creation.

When we think of the garden of Eden, we see God's original plan for man. It was a happy plan. He designed everything happy. Adam and Eve's days were happy as they communed with nature and with God. The garden was an amazing site to behold. Imagine the vivid green plants, the crisp blue sky, the plush carpet of grass, and the laughter shared as they played with the birds and the animals. Really, imagine. What could be more joyful than a funny little squirrel or a baby rabbit? God has expectations of creation, that is purpose.

The joy of the Lord is a source of happiness. It allows us to find happiness in our relationship with him and others. It also allows us to find contentment within creation and within the realms of the spirit. For this reason, every person desires to be happy. Not one of us wants to be unhappy. That's because God is the ultimate source of happiness and not only that, he is happiness. Let that sink in. God is happy. So why is happiness important to the point that people will do almost anything for it? Well, I'm glad you asked.

Within the depths of our being, we know that joy, happiness, and gladness are necessary for a prosperous body, soul, and spirit. It is essential to a flourishing life. Laughter is the expression of happiness and a powerful key to a fulfilling life. The fundamental truth to all that has been said and all that will be said in this book is that laughter helps our soul to prosper and when our soul prospers everything about us prospers, but we cannot fully experience prosperity in God until we know him as the only true source of happiness.

Beloved, I wish above all things that thou mayest prosper and be in health, even as thy soul prospereth.
—3 John 2

In this scripture, John is writing to the church, com- mending them for walking in the truth. That scripture is the whole point of this book. The truth is that God is the God of joy. He created you to live a life of abundant joy and happiness.

These things have I spoken unto you, that my joy might remain in you, and that your joy might be full.
—John 15:11 KJV

In this scripture, Jesus is helping his followers understand the relationship between God and them. He expresses that he wants them to understand so they will abide in overflowing joy. According to Google defines joy as "a feeling of great pleasure and happiness." I hope you are getting this. God wants us to be happy! Happiness brings prosperity, good health in our bodies, and a soul that is whole.

According to health and wellness specialist Carol Rundle, the following is true. To be prosperous can be defined as, "to have a successful journey."

A successful journey is what most people want. They want things to work out and their dreams to come true. They want their plans to succeed. To many, happiness is money in the bank. To others happiness is having love in their life. Jesus tells us that understanding and abiding in a right relation- ship with God is the key to overflowing joy.

To be in health can be defined as having "nothing missing and nothing broken" in your natural existence.

So, we see that being prosperous is to have good success, but to be in health is to have everything fixed. This includes being well in body and having what is necessary for personal maintenance and well-being.

To have a prosperous soul is to have a soul that is "fed with nourishment from God." This produces the peace that surpasses understanding and a heart that focuses on those things which are good.

The Lord says that our thoughts are not his thoughts and our ways not his ways. I believe that is the reason so few people see joy in God.

There are those who perceive that God is a God of laughter and they are able to benefit from the happiness that is an innate part of God. As we have just discussed, happiness is truly what God wants for us. He wants us to be successful while we are here on Earth. He wants us to have a healthy body, experience healthy relationships, and possess all that we need to experience a life that is complete in him. Most importantly, he wants us to experience a close connection to him. If you are close enough to God, he will, when you least expect it, reach over and tickle your funny bone.

GOD HAS PROMISED TO MAKE YOU LAUGH

Till he [shall] fill thy mouth with laughing, and thy lips with rejoicing.

—Job 8:21 KJV

Then was our mouth filled with laughter, and our tongue with singing: then said they among the heathen, the Lord hath done great things for them.

—Psalm 126:2 KJV

Blessed are ye that hunger now: for ye shall be filled. Blessed are ye that weep now: for ye shall laugh.

—Luke 6:21 KJV

Let's look at Job in a season of great affliction. It is so bad that his friend begins to accuse Job of being the cause of what is perceived as God's punishment on Job for some sin Job has committed. Job's friend reasons that Job must have done something. Anyone who knows, this story knows that Job was having a hard time, not because he had done wrong, but because he was a super achiever. The Bible says,

> There lived in the land of Uza man named Job—a good man who feared

God and stayed away from evil. He had
a large family of seven sons and three
daughters and was immensely wealthy,
for he owned 7,000 sheep, 3,000
camels, 500 teams of oxen, 500 fe- male
donkeys, and employed many servants.
He was, in fact, the richest cattleman in
that entire area.

—Job 1:1–3 TLB

By all accounts, Job was very rich and near perfect
in the sight of God. Job's friends didn't have a clue
about Job's real relationship with God, so they just
came up with what made sense to them.

Many times, life doesn't make sense, does it? There
are seasons in life when things seem like they are
never going to work out. And, to add insult to in- jury,
family, friends, co-workers, and even people we barely
associate with have something negative to say. They
jump to judgements and even outright fabrications just
to perpetuate a conversation about what is (or is not)
the reality of your life. The bad thing about it is that
it is during these times that we need encouragement
the most. The Word of God proclaims that the joy of
the Lord is our strength. When do we need strength
the most? We need God's strength when we are the
weakest.

Job's friends got it wrong when it came to Job, but
got it right when it came to the character of God. I
guess they didn't want Job to feel totally hopeless, so
they made an effort to make him feel a little better
having falsely accused him at first. They told him God
wouldn't let him stay down forever. Glory to God!

Since you are reading this book, God has a message specifically for you. He wants you to know that he won't let you stay down forever. Whether you are experiencing a disheartening challenge right now or not, the important thing is to raise your awareness about the personality of God. He is the one who brings us up and out of various negative situations and he is the one who puts a smile on our face.

In Psalm 126:3 KJV, we see God restoring the joy of Zion to the point that they exclaim, "The Lord hath done great things for us; whereof we are glad."

In Luke 6:21 KJV, Jesus taught his disciples by sharing wisdom he knew they would need in the future. Jesus had finished healing a big crowd of people. He didn't only heal some of them, but all of them. He looked up at his disciples and told them, "Blessed are ye that hunger now: for ye shall be filled. Blessed are ye that weep now: for ye shall laugh."

In each of these three scriptures, we see a theme developing. A mystery is being exposed. God's way is to restore happiness in the lives of those who are downtrodden. We have to recognize his goodness. Right now, take a moment to look introspectively into your own life. Think about anything you have lost, any trauma you have experienced, or any trying situation you have faced. What is it? What have been the effects? Like Job, have you hit rock bottom and then suffered as people ostracized you in the face of your pain. Are you or someone you know a part of a collective that is often oppressed? Such oppressed groups can include the poor, the disabled, women, or even Christians who are treated unfairly because of their faith. Do you have a ministry to help people who need help? Does their pain wrench at your heart? These are the scenarios described in previous scrip- tures. In each of them, God takes those who are down and lifts them up. He not only improves their lives but puts laughter into their souls. He is the God of your laughter.

The spirit of joy is rising up even as you are reading these pages. The spirit of joy comes not only to make you laugh, but it's power comes to defeat your enemies, heal your body, manifest your God-given desires, and change your situation. If only you could see that God is laughing at your problems because your problems think they are bigger than he is. He is waiting on you to start laughing too. This does not mean that our Father takes our difficulties lightly. No, not at all. He sees the victory at the end. He's laughing at our defeated foe who's trying to win a bat- tle he's already lost. Yes, by faith we laugh because the victory was won on Calvary.

Chapter Two

My Laughter
Is A Weapon

I dream so much. I am amazed how my dreams have blessed me and so many others. On March 22, 2018, I woke up grinning as my legs were moving to their own dance. In the dream, I was at a huge worship ser- vice where the songs were so powerful. I remember trying to wave the leader down to get his attention, even though he was still singing. No one would call me a professional singer, but I have lead devotional services and testimonial services at my home church for more than four years. I love the songs like "We've Come to Glorify His Name," "I Feel More Deter- mined," "My Soul Says Yes," "His Eye is On the Spar- row," and so many more. If you are not familiar with these songs, you are missing out on some powerful worship music. As they continued to sing in my dream, they were singing "My Praise Is A Weapon!" My God! My God! There was so much fire in that song. I was thrilled when the microphone was passed to me. I started singing, "My Laughter is a Weapon." Everyone caught on singing and laughing—at first laughing at my voice, then laughing with me in the spirit. People were running up sharing with the pas- tor about what they had gotten healed or delivered from. The spirit of joy comes not only to make you laugh, but it's power comes to heal your body, change your situation, manifest your God-given desires, and defeat your enemies. Laughter gives life. I am not making light of the pain of your situation, but what I am saying is that in the midst of our worst problems, the devil expects us to crumble. I clearly heard the Lord say to me "you cried, but you didn't crumble." That will preach all day any day. So many times I felt like giving up, but not only would the Lord bring me out, but he would bring me out with so much joy. The stories of how he brought me out were too funny not to be God. My laughter became my weapon.

THIS WEAPON HAS THE POWER TO HEAL

I am reminded of the well-known story of a man named Norman Cousins who was diagnosed with a painful degenerative disease, rendering him bedridden and unable to use his extremities. The condition was extremely painful and no medicine could alleviate it. The doctors gave him only months to live. Having run out of options, Mr. Cousins decided to try laughter as a means of getting relief. The more he prompted himself to laugh, the more he recovered. After approximately 24 months of healing-laughter, he was restored.

What a powerful testimony of God's goodness. I am not sure whether Mr. Cousins was a believer in the Lord Jesus Christ, but as the story goes, he surmised that if stress and negativity contributed to his condition then laughter and positive emotions could restore him. It did. The Word of God says, "A merry heart doeth good like a medicine: but a broken spirit drieth the bones (Proverbs 17:22 KJV).

God is our healer. Blessed is the person who puts their trust in God. He gives good gifts to his children. Regardless of Mr. Cousins' position, I know God is a healer. His Word clearly speaks of the healing virtues of laughter. That being said, let me digress for just a moment.

Praise and worship are powerful in that they charge the atmosphere with the presence of God. The Bible says that God dwells (manifests) in the praises of his people. How do we know when God 'shows up'? We know because of the signs and wonders that fol- low. When God shows up people receive Christ as their Savior. Many are healed, demons are cast out, some people sense his peace, tormenting thoughts leave, inspiration comes, praise increases, unity comes, and many other manifestations too numerous to name.

In thy presence is fullness of joy; at thy right hand there are pleasures for evermore.

—Psalm 16:11 KJV

One common thread in most manifestations of God's presence is joy. That says a lot right there. The light of God drives out the darkness. Where God is present, sickness and disease have no grounds to stand. When we sense the joy of the Lord (his presence), it is okay to laugh. It won't take God two years to heal you when you come into alignment with him. Laugh out loud right now. Say, "Devil, you have been defeated by the shed blood of Jesus Christ, and this sickness in my body, mind, heart, or spirit (wherever and whatever it may be) has already been healed. Get out!" Just laugh at the Devil and tell the Lord: "Thank you." The next thing you know, the pain is gone, your broken heart is mended, and there will only be peace in your heart, mind, and soul. Glory to God!

MAN WAS CREATED FOR JOY

One of the ways we can know man was created for joy is by taking another look at the garden of Eden. This was the first paradise created for humanity. Imagine a plush overabundance of everything. Beautiful animals, vegetation, and rolling hills filled with magnificent streams of water are what I picture. However the garden was situated, it was designed with Adam's happiness in mind. Then, if that were not enough, God created Eve. Take a moment to meditate on the creation of Eve. What is it in life that a man could want more than a good woman—don't distort what I am trying to say. We all know there are people who are disinterested in the opposite sex for reasons too numerous to name. Nevertheless, most people desire a mate that is compatible to them above all else. Most people dream of creating a paradise of love with their husband or wife, believing that the other person will make them happy. The point is that God created Eden and gave Eve to Adam, which was by all ac- counts the ultimate paradise. Why? My answer is that God created man for joy. He wanted Adam and Eve to be exceedingly happy.

HAPPY COMPARED TO STRESSED

Being happy has been equated with being contented, radiant, elated, jubilant, and even tickled pink. When we read these words, the feeling we get is a good feeling. Our subconscious mind and spirit know without question that 'happy' and all the synonyms that go with it are a part of our original design. In fact we were designed to start in joy (live in Eden) and end in joy (spend eternity in heaven). This is God's only design. There is no plan B for humanity as far as God is concerned.

On the other hand, there is an opposite. That opposite is stress. The Bible speaks of man toiling by the sweat of his brow. This is not a part of God's original design. For this reason, we must conclude that stress is unnatural to the spirit, soul (which includes the mind), or body.

Just as with being happy, there are numerous ways to describe being stressed. However, there are two words that best sum up stress—pressure and tension. A little of either of these can be good. Some say they keep us sharp. Stress in excess causes a host of physical disorders such as backaches, heart attacks, and high blood pressure. Unfortunately, it doesn't stop there. A steady diet of stress will cause negative soulish responses as well, such as fear, worry, and hopelessness. This impacts your spiritual responses that involve rejecting the provisions of God—joy, peace, happiness, salvation, healing; all basic needs, and God's plan for a blessed existence in both the natural and spiritual realm.

There are situations that promote stress. One of the biggest issues is the constant lies that the Devil speaks. There is also physical torment, lack of re- sources, loss, deferred hope, lack of love, mental torment, not having a father or family, believing there is no God or that God does not care, or carrying your own burdens. Even greater issues could be, working in your own strength. Whether in school or on your job, trying to solve problems on your own can be stressful. When we fail to utilize the power and wisdom of the Holy Spirit, we stir up a natural recipe for stress.

It doesn't take a rocket scientist or a brain surgeon to know that people were not designed for constant stress, but rather, God made man for joy. As we come into the realization of this fact, our actions will begin to follow our beliefs. Even if a person does not know God personally, if they realize they were not de- signed for all this stress, based on their enhanced ide- ology, their subconscious will begin to lead them into a less stressful more fulfilling life.

Listen, let's keep it real, do I laugh all the time, no ma'am and no sir, but I have the joy of the Lord. It has been the weapon to fight against discouragements and heartache. If the world developed laugh clinics, how can we as people of God ignore the importance and benefit of laughter?

If we want to experience the laughter of God, we have to be reconciled back to God. Let's face it, we have all sinned and come short of the Glory of God. Sin has separated humanity from God, thus separating us from the original design of God. Don't live a life of hellish stress and unhappiness now only to go to hell later. God wants to put laughter back in your life. This reminds me of an old song I heard titled, "He Brought Laughter into My Soul." This traditional African-American song makes the claim that it would have been enough, if he [God] brought life. It further states that having brought peace and joy would have been sufficient as well. I think we can all say that we are grateful that God did not stop there—"he brought laughter into my soul."

GENERAL BENEFITS OF LAUGHTER—YOUR WEAPON

It is said that laughter has a positive effect on the physical, mental, and spiritual aspects of our life.

Here are a few physical benefits:

- increase in life expectancy
- decrease in stress hormones
- more efficient burning of calories and aid to the immune system

Some of the mental health benefits are:

- easier to let go of anger
- teamwork and other social skills are promoted
- a healthy boldness is encouraged

The spiritual or supernatural benefits of laughing are many. I have listed several, but if you think about it, there are probably far more.

- When we laugh in the face of great difficulty, it causes divine outcomes to materialize.
- When we laugh at sickness, a supernatural healing takes place.
- When we laugh at poverty and financial hardships, unexpected resources appear.
- When we laugh in the face of impossible situations, what was once hard becomes easy.
- When we laugh in the face of fear, we become very bold.
- When we laugh in the face of long-term difficulties, speedy breakthroughs take place.
- When we laugh in the face of lying spirits, we shut their mouths.
- When we laugh in the face of mocking spirits, they are brought to open shame.
- When we laugh in the face of the spirit of death, angels drive it back to the deep.
- When we laugh in the face of the spirit of anti-Christ, the defiled ones become cleansed.
- When we laugh in the face of witchcraft, dark forces become confused.

- When we laugh at incomplete projects, the rust is removed and we finish quickly.
- When we laugh in the face of stress, peace is soon to come.
- When we laugh in the face of danger, we become aware of God's protection.
- When we laugh in the face of disappointment, we receive double.
- When we laugh at rejection, love materializes from human and spiritual sources.
- When we laugh at tormenting spirits, judgement befalls demons affecting the mind.
- When we laugh at our enemies, it is because we are prophesying their defeat.
- When we laugh in the face of danger, we become aware of God's protection.
- When we laugh at tormenting spirits, judgement befalls demons affecting the mind.
- When we laugh at hopelessness, grace comes in large waves.
- When God laughs at our enemies, destruction befalls them quickly. Yes, laughter is a powerful weapon.

CHAPTER THREE

IT'S TOO FUNNY NOT TO BE GOD

Now that you've read the first two chapters, hopefully you have a better understanding of how God is a God of joy and laughter. Personally, I believe laughter is the sound of joy and smiling is one way to wear joy. The things that you are experiencing today, God knows the power and strength of joy we need. I invite you to get a Bible story in your mind that seems ra- ther comical, like the donkey talking or the axe head floating on water. I want you to lighten up and say out loud with me, "It's too funny not to be God!" or maybe, think about some of your own personal experiences.

Have you ever been getting ready for a very important meeting, and not be able to find your keys? Allow me to say to all the folks like me, "I always put myself there." We are looking at the clock and looking for the keys, then we start talking to Lord, ourselves or anybody around, "Where are my keys? I just had them!" Then you hear, "Go back and look," and then you find them! This is really funny (strange), but we thank God and just maybe we say like my mom used to say, "That's nobody but God," then my momma would get so tickled. In some instances she would say "Couldn't nobody have done that but God!" With my momma, it wasn't keys because she didn't drive, but her comments of gratitude would be heard in whatever she needed God to do for her. When he answered, she would be full of joy.

I firmly believe that every victory is coupled with joy. Oh come on, think about it, why is it when good things happens we want to celebrate, whether it be a new job, engagement, pregnancy, passing an exam, etc. If you really think about it, laughter is present at these special times. Yes indeed, God brings laughter to our soul. Expect the laughter. It is a bonus. You can have the victory with joy and laughter. With that laughter, you receive the real medicine you need.

The more we are able to recognize God in those situations, the more we are able to testify and give him the glory. When we allow the funny (strange) way that God sometimes works us out of our problems, it prompts us to laughter.

I have discovered that the more aware we are of the way God operates, the less likely we are to miss our instructions that lead to our blessings.

Listen, it's not about where I live, what I drive, or how I dress, I still need help in all of those areas. I am writing about what I have lived through in hope that this knowledge will be used to help you on your journey. My knowledge became my strength and my refusal to be destroyed from the lack there of. There have been too many days and nights filled with tears, sadness, depression, shame, rejection, loneliness, fear, and sickness. And yes, my keeping-it-real list could go on. The funny (difficult to explain or under- stand; strange) thing about it, I was married. That is a story all by itself, the point is, your status doesn't exempt you from the attacks of the enemy, it doesn't matter if you are rich, poor, black, white, young, old, married, singled, divorced, etc., the next lines are for you. Take your joy back and enjoy your time. It is not about a superficial 'ha ha' or being 'fake.' God wants our joy to be filled until it runs over into laughter.

As far back as 2007, I shared more with three of my friends (Bettie M, Paris D, and Michaele B.) than I did with any other friends—testimony after testimony of how I would ask God for an answer and he would tell me to do something that seemed to be totally opposite to the answer I was looking for. The results would leave me nearly speechless. But, obedience, obedience! Look at Gideon and his army in Judges 7, God told Gideon to keep the ones who lapped like a dog? Really?

When I would tell my friend Michaele B., she would laugh so hard and say me, "Girl you need to write a book." One day I asked her if I wrote a book what would I called it? She said, "It's too funny not to be God." Even though it took a long time before I got started on it, I could never get it out of my mind because she would repeat it over and over. Her words made me more aware of God's presence and that laughter was in the midst of his answers to me.

It wasn't until January 2018, I called a local pastor in Memphis, to inquire about possibly using one of his facilities for my first writer's conference scheduled for June 23, 2018. As he understood what the event was, he immediately told me about one of his members who is an author. I'm glad I took his suggestion. This story is too funny not to be God. Keep in mind I was planning for a writer's conference and I had no clue that I would be writing this book in 2018. After a phone meeting with the woman this pastor recommended, I soon learned that she was an author of multiple books. In turn, she suggested I meet with Dell Self, a book project manager for those who wish to self-publish. Now, Dell is the project manager for my book. Look at God!

In this chapter, as you are feeling a little lighter and your endorphins have been stimulated through laughter, I trust that the title has caused you to see God in your life in a different way. And if you don't, you cannot miss chapter four because I have asked others to share personal stories just for you!

On May 9, 2018, I was talking to Dell about the title I had chosen for this chapter. She quietly listened, then I asked what she thought about it. This phenomenal woman of God calmly began to share her experience. After reading her story and the others in this chapter, take a break, then come back because you don't want to miss the powerful and awesome sharing of others in chapter four. Since they were written just for you, you might as well stay in here to the finish.

The Orange Dress

A few weeks ago, while decluttering a closet, I came across an orange dress. I wondered why I had the dress and why in such a hideous color. I tried it on even though I had every intention of either giving or throwing it away. Oddly enough, the dress fit quite nicely. I took it off, placed it with the other items to be removed from the house, and gave it no more thought. The following week, a friend (and business associate) had a scheduling conflict and needed me to sit in for her at a conference. As she gave all the details, I was preparing my rationale to avoid going because I was working on a book project. She concluded her informational spiel with, "... and everyone has to wear orange." My jaw dropped—only God. What are the odds of me finding an orange dress (that fits), a few days before I am requested to wear or-ange? Yes, sometimes things are too funny not to be God. And yes, my orange dress and I went to the con-ference.

Dell Self

It's Too Funny Not To Be God

Brenda! Brenda! Brenda! I have to take a deep breath just to calm myself down from all the craziness and miraculous events that have taken place since coming to know you. At first, I just observed your spiritual walk from a distance. It was seemingly normal. You and your sweetness seemed to be the ideal loving, spiritual couple in ministry with well-behaved children. Beautiful.

I truly believed in your ministry because the Word of God was so emphasized and profound. It kept my heart encouraged. Of course, this again was from a distance, not up close and personal.

Up close and personal came as a result of things happening in the church when I was an outsider and believed, laughingly, that they sent you to spy me out. You were not a good spy because you got too close and became my lean on, go to, informational person.

God forged a friendship/kinship that was unforeseeable by all. The miracles and things that God was doing in your life were so insane, causing us to cry and laugh saying, "It's too funny not to be God!"

Starting off with the miracle of the computer revealing folks' movements in another city, to the millionaire woman on the plane, to shopping with very little money ("Come buy without money ...") is so true in your life that it certainly causes me to 'grab a holt' to more faith. You have great faith! Your faith is greater than mine though, 'cause I still have to make sure I have enough money to get what I want. Not you. You wait on God to tell you where and/or when to go and he would have already paved the way.

Your life is a funny book that God has authored. I know that everyone who reads it will be reading an epistle straight from God by way of Brenda, chapter 22. No doubts.

With much love and as you say, "All is well! Mmm hummm."

Michaele Byers

LAUGHTER IN A RELATIONSHIP
The Diane and Brenda Story

When God uses laughter to enhance a relationship it usually lasts forever. When we laugh together we al- ways repeat the motion again and again to recreate the memory. The sense of humor God uses can be quite embarrassing sometimes. However, if you know who you are and the persons you're with allows you the freedom to be you, the relationship becomes a joyful life long journey. The smallest things become a collection of sentimental value.

The soil it takes to grow a relationship is poured into the heart of the jars filled with love, peace, bold- ness, strength, tears, pain, and mountains of apologies. The relationship then converts into an unending season of blooms.

Lifelong relationships are daily discoveries. Gently we walk miles in the same shoes knowing all the while it may not always be easy, but such is life itself. Life undresses us to prove we are one and the same. We are never ashamed of the road we've traveled. Still, we hold on to the prize trophy of a lifelong relationship. Now you will carry one shoe and I will al- ways carry the other. Wait, which shoe do you have, the left or the right? Does it really matter?

Diane Norwood

ALL IN ONE CALL

It is a great privilege and honor to be a small part of this awesome project. Brenda is a very special per- son. We met on the telephone. From our first conversation, I knew there was something different about her. Our business together quickly transitioned into a strong friendship. I had no idea that our seemingly chance encounter was actually a divine connection.

God knows the end from the beginning. We see the beginning at the end. Then, we realize that God had been directing our path all along. What seemed like coincidences of life, were really acts of God orchestrating our destiny.

A couple of years ago, I was browsing in a store when a piece of wall art caught my eye. I did not need it, but I felt compelled, so I bought it. I hung it in my office. Fast forward. I was talking to Brenda and she told me she was hosting a writer's conference in June. I was ecstatic with anticipation. Fast forward again. During one of our telephone conversations, Brenda was describing her office. She sent me a picture of her office table. I hollered and immediately sent her a picture of the plaque on my wall. She had the same reaction. The plaque said, "Write your own life's story."

I had never shared with Brenda that one of my life goals is to write. Brenda asked me to help her; but God was using her to bless me. I am forever grateful that Brenda allowed God to use her. I smile when I think of how my life has been changed for the better— all in one call.

Addie Burks

CHAPTER FOUR

IT LOOKS PERSONAL, BUT IT'S POWERFUL

I asked the Lord how was I going to write a book and do a writers' conference in the same year with only four months to finish the book. In November 2017, the Lord reminded me of a dream I had in 2006. At the time, I really didn't pay too much attention to it. February 2018, as I was praying about taking on this book writing assignment, the Father reminded me of that same dream, again. This year, I had that dream in January, but when I woke up this time, I could hear part of the scripture found in Ephesians 4:16 KJV. All I heard was "fitly joined together ... every joint supplieth the other." Immediately, I realized that was my answer to how I was going to complete this book, it was all in the dream.

Wow! This is truly another example of it's too funny not to be God. As strange as it sounds, it bears me sharing the dream.

I had a dream that I was sitting at a table with some of my friends around me. At some point they reached out to me. I extended my right arm and they made contact with me some sort of way. Some were touching my hand, arm, fingers, elbow, or my shoulder. Once everyone had made contact, each of our hands lit up. I know this sounds like something from the movie ET. I thought the same thing—it sounded like somebody was under some type of influence. This year, the revelation of the dream was very clear when I heard "every joint supplieth the other." The Lord clearly said to me, "Ask your family and friends these four questions":

1. If they had to choose between reading and writing, which would they choose?
2. Did they have a story to share that goes along with this title, a funny situation that ended in victory?
3. Did they have a moment in their life when they knew it was dark, but the Lord came and delivered them out of it?
4. Do they have a declaration or prophetic word they would like to share?

I would only listen to two or maybe three lines, then God would drop a title for their writing in my spirit (except for one person).

I pray the following writings in this chapter encourage you to no end. It is always good to hear testimonies from others as they tell personally, what they have been through. Those I was able to reach gladly contributed to be a blessing to you and others in excellence. I was blessed by what I finally got to read and I appreciate them for keeping it real. The number of contributors grew daily, but I did not hear God say to stop anyone. Some heard what was going on and asked if they could be a part. I wasn't going to stop them because I knew God was up to something bigger than me. I knew he had you in mind.

Each person responded to a request even though they weren't really sure what they were doing. Still they stepped out in faith at my word. I couldn't tell them fully what I was doing because I was stepping out in faith at God's word. Yes indeed, it looks personal. It looks like a lot of people I know or have crossed my path recently.

I love good healthy relationships, even though I had to realize the power of God in how he orchestrated this chapter for you. My soul still leaps inside me. It didn't make sense at first. From the title of this book to the chapter you are reading now, I know it's God. Many times as I would go through, I didn't feel like reading the Bible, I would pick up anything to read to take my mind off of what was happening to me. If I didn't read, I would write. Each of my children remembers the countless notebooks, journals, and notepads they've seen around the house. It's funny, as they were moving out, I was blessed to see they kept the notebooks and such.

In this chapter, you will see how others have

expressed how reading or writing helped them just in case you think this chapter does not fit or make a lot of sense. Trust me, keep reading. Hopefully my obedience in inserting this chapter will remind you of the things he has told you that didn't make sense—things like walking around a car lot praying, claiming a house with no "For Sale" sign outside, picking out names and baby clothes before the pregnancy, stand- ing in the mirror answering a make-believe phone with the title of a job you don't have yet, setting the table for two even though you're still single, shouting and dancing for your healing when the doctors just told you have cancer, calling out your children's names thanking God for their ministries while they are still out in the world doing all sorts of things, or buying a new ink pen, and acting like you're writing checks when your account has a negative balance. I could go on and on because I have lived through most of it. Save your breath. I'm the wrong person to talk to about what doesn't make sense when it comes to obeying God. I just want you to get on board.

When I started to write this book, I was certain I was going to tell of all the stories I have been sharing with my family and friends. God told me to allow others to share their stories instead. I did and I don't regret it.

Since I have been asked a number of times, how I knew I was supposed to write this book, I will answer with one of my shortest and funniest stories. This story is about when my youngest son and his family were leaving to move to Georgia. I knew I needed to say my goodbyes. It was the day I planned to get my nails done—I can tell they were tired having to man- age a little baby with another one on the way. I asked if there was anything they wanted me to do. My son said, "Well, do you mind taking my car to get the oil changed before we hit the road?" Can somebody re- peat the question for me, out loud, again? That re- quest made little sense to me. In my mind, he might as well have asked me to load all the boxes in the truck for him. This request required that I drive from Arkansas back to the dealership in Memphis. I did ask, so of course I said, "Yes." Once I got to the dealer- ship and pulled on to the lot, I saw a big sign outside that read, "Nails Done Free with an Oil Change." I couldn't stop laughing and taking pictures. Only God!

I began talking with some other ladies about this deal we were getting regarding getting our nails done for free. We had never heard of such a thing.

The conversation stayed lively, but with one woman in particular, we talked beyond the manicure. I remember so clearly, when I asked her name, she said, "Ann Lawson." The next thing she said had to be God. She then said, "You should write." That was my second confirmation. We continued to talk, then, she asked me to wait while she went to her car. She came back and gave me her book. No, that's not the end of the story. God was working and connecting dots. We continued to talk. I told her what church I went to and then she smiled and told me that her best friend, Ola Miller, goes there and I told her that her friend is my big sister in the Lord. Now that's too funny not to be God!

As you continue to turn these pages, you will see time and time again that many of life's experiences are simply too funny not to be God.

Court To Courtship

I'm sitting on the pew with my cousin and a police officer, while Ben is in the pulpit about to deliver his first sermon. It is a miracle that I'm here because I promised myself I'd never consider dating a minister. However, my cousin worked with Ben and heard the Holy Spirit tell her to invite me to hear him. At the end of service, we were introduced, shook hands, the end, or so we thought. Two weeks later (while in a traffic ticket line), who do I see? It's Benjamin coming toward me. We knew then that it was a divine connection. I thought, "For real God? From court to courtship; this is too funny not to be God." A whole year prior, my dad broke my tail light by backing into a garbage can resulting in a traffic ticket set 3 months out to place me at Ben's job two weeks after his first sermon. Funnier than that, I was invited to church by a police officer to meet Ben and sent to court by police officers and met Ben again. Ultimately, a broken tail light, a word from God, and court date strategically orchestrated by our heavenly Father, worked together to create a love story titled "From Court to Courtship."

Angie Allen

THE WRITE TO EXHALE

Indeed, "it is in him that we move, breathe, and have our very being." Within our "being" or temple in which we are housed, our humanity breathes; inhal- ing and exhaling. Physically, more effort is used to breathe in (inhale), than is used to breathe out (ex- hale). In life, we inhale volumes.

Our defense mechanism (immune system) is constantly at work. There are moments that the intake of our encounters outweigh the comprehension and perception of those experiences and we're left with "taking those things that remain" to make sense of it all. Sometimes, it actually makes no sense.

What do I do when I've inhaled something that yields no clarity, whereby my physical, emotional, social, psychological, and spiritual defenses calculate no answer within the purview of that very present moment? I can't tell this. No, I can't tell anybody that will believe me without questioning my intelligence or in- vestigating further to ensure that there's no change in my mental status. Oh, yes—I've had crazy on top of crazy where I could only tell God and to ensure personal release of residual pressure, I let the paper suffer the consequences, allowing as much ink as possible to reach down into the depth, devouring the core-induced experience to become merely a shadow through writing, for I have "the write to exhale."

J. E. Barnes

From Hole To Held

The hole was deep. Depression started one day, then lasted weeks, then months, and eventually years. For me, it started at age 11 when I was told that my father had been killed. No explanation. He was gone. I lived for years wondering why my family would tell me that. Depression came to live with me, like a hole. The hole grew when I was raped. I felt that it might not have happened if my father had been there to help. I loved my father. Deep inside, I knew it was not his fault.

As an adult, my hole continued to grow. I longed to be free. Life had not been my friend. I got saved, married, and had kids, yet depression remained my constant companion. But God said to me through Psalm 61:2 KJV (paraphrased), "From the end of the earth I call to you, when your heart is overwhelmed and weak," and it was. "Stephanie, I will lead you to the rock that is higher than your pain."

Healing from depression takes more than time. It takes intentionality, courage, and humility. You have to do the work that freedom demands. Let God rescue you from the enemy. I pray that as you climb out your hole of depression, you will climb into the arms of our Savior and delight in being held by the one who loves your more than you could ever imagine. He is the only one who can bring you from the hole to being held in his loving arms.

Stephanie Y. Becton

READING BRINGS LIFE

Have you ever read a book, a quote, or the Bible and immediately felt refreshed? You, my friend have been the recipient of an impartation, more like a deposit, of life. There is a T-shirt, designed by Redbubble, which reads "Reading Gives Life More Life."

As you make your book selections, be willing to take a journey through the eyes of the author. Whether it be the Word of God, a secular book that challenges you to elevate your thoughts, or a letter from a friend; take a moment and use godly wisdom to open your spirit and receive life. Awaken and live.

Abundant life is ours and reading is just one avenue by which God allows us to experience this life in a profound way. As you read this book, I pray light and life flow into your situation. May every stagnant place begin to flow free and unhindered. Allow read- ing to bring life to your life.

Salina A. Carter

WHAT SHALL I DO?

So, what shall I do when my circumstances are sending me into the abyss of chaos?

So, what shall I do when I cannot seem to make sense of my life?

So, what shall I do when I realize that I have a habit of making wrong decisions?

So, what shall I do when I have not answered the yearning in my gut? The yearning that rises up more than every now and again. You know the feeling; when you see that another "unknown" has started a business, written a blog, opened a restaurant, started a ministry, or written a best seller.

So, what shall I do when I feel like I waited too late to share my gift because of fear? Does it mean that I no longer possess that gift or it is not relevant anymore?

So, what shall I do when I realize that I am stuck in the pattern of fear and procrastination?

So, what shall I do when I realize that I have not prayed, declared or taken a step towards clarity?

I will meditate, murmur, pray, believe and follow the God's instructions below.

1 Corinthians 14:15

So, what shall I do? I will pray with my spirit, but I will also pray with my mind. I will sing with my spirit, but I will also sing with my mind.

So, what shall I do? I will pray, dance and sing with delight and joy as I go from chaos to clarity!

I will remember that I am leaving my chaos with laughter at the enemy of my soul; and I will rejoice because I now know what to do!

Paris Ducker

The Blessing In Writing

In life, there are people that express their feelings better through writing than verbal communication.

Whether spiritual or natural, there's something about a written word that can pierce your heart.

When the response to what I write is, "Your words helped me," "That was uplifting," or "That was encouraging," I see that as a reflection of the power of the written word.

At a revival I attended, the visiting pastor was teaching on faith and healing. The result: God healed me.

I wrote a letter to the pastor sharing my testimony that I had received a super-natural healing. The pastor was ecstatic. He shared the letter with congregations and people all over the world. They believed that since the Lord healed me, he would heal them as well.

Thirty years later, I received a call from that pastor's wife stating, "I still have the letter you wrote. Many people have heard your testimony, but I am requesting your permission to give a copy of your letter to someone suffering from the same health challenge you had." Although surprised by her request, I was grateful to God, after all these years my written testimony could still impact the lives of others. To God be the Glory!

Lady Fran

How To Get Stoned At A Camp Meeting

In 1998, Bob and I were seeking something from God which we did not even understand. Even though we watched international evangelist Perry Stone on television, we never heard that "something" for which we were looking. His program ended with an invitation to come to a "camp meeting" in Pigeon Forge, TN. My ex-Catholic husband and his Southern Baptist wife from Ohio went ready to 'camp.'

We entered the conference center on a warm spring day as anyone would going to 'camp,' Bob in shorts and sandals and I in a sundress. We were escorted to the front (we always sat in the front), under the surprised look of hundreds of attendees dressed in their Sunday best. When Perry came in, it didn't take but a second for him to notice the two people obviously out of place. He looked us up and down and kept glancing our way the entire service. Little did we realize that God was orchestrating a divine appointment.

He spoke about the Baptism of the Holy Spirit (repeating the declaration we spoke to God on our drive down), gave an invitation, we accepted, and our lives were changed forever. Not only that, but we became great friends and continue to laugh at how God can bring people together. Indeed, we left that camp meeting "Stoned."

Bob and Cheryl Gesing

A Continuous Calm

No matter how my day starts, no matter what I faced the day before, no matter how my night unfolds, when I begin to write it shines like gold. There's a calm, a sense of satisfaction and productivity that takes over. It supersedes life's day-to-day issues. Whether Sunday school books, sermons, poetry, plays, or daily reading it releases the same peace. When the Lord starts speaking, I start writing. There is no second-guessing how it should sound or who would be positively affected. The movement of the Spirit intercedes and the words begin to flow like milk and honey. It's as if I had reached the throne room and at the feet of Jesus with a spoon in my hand. My history and experiences all become posi- tive. It seems as though my mistakes in life are now pieces to a puzzle that are being revealed. In this place of calmness, I find no insecurities or fault in myself, only a willingness to obey. My spoon never comes back empty and each time I raise it for more, I'm never rejected or disappointed. I encourage every reader to raise their spoon not for only motivating others, but for personal gratification as well. Scribes of God, be blessed as you bless others.

Diane Givens

OFF THE SHELF

Often times in life, we are placed in situations and circumstances where it seems as if we're forever waiting on the manifestation of open doors. Waiting often tests our faith and tries our character. Sometimes it even places us in a low place where at times we question why things aren't happening the way we thought or planned? Have you considered the Bible story of Joseph? He was a favored, faithful, and upright man. When he tried to make the best of one situation, there arose another obstacle. However, it was his circumstances that placed him on the shelf of God's perfect timing. As Joseph waited on God, he was being pre- pared and reconstructed at the same time. Perhaps that's what your wait has been about. God has been preparing you to elevate you. When something is elevated it is raised or lifted to a higher position. How- ever, elevation must first start from a low place then a lift can occur. Joseph's lift came suddenly through Pharaoh. In an instance, Joseph was taken off the shelf of waiting and elevated into the open door of his calling. Now is the time to believe and expect every- thing you've been praying for to manifest. In God's magnificent timing, you'll be taken off the shelf and used mightily.

Lisa Head

THE KISS

The sudden jolt of widowhood officially marked the beginning of my new millennium. It had been predicted that Y2K would create havoc as year 2000 entered. But soon after, my world was shattered by the unexpected loss of my 49-year-old husband. It meant no taking our son off to college together, no growing old and travelling together, no sharing stories with grandchildren and no future that resembled anything ever dreamed. Instead, day-to-day survival became my theme.

Months into grieving, I began the practice of walking and meditating early morning, before the heat enveloped the day. With my trusty dog, I would imagine that I was walking in God's garden, enjoying his handiwork without the intrusion of anything manmade. The sights, sounds, smells, and touch of God's natural world brought me a renewed appreciation for life.

One very still morning, while reflecting on what the Lord had spoken to me two days before my husband's death, a sudden, gentle breeze—a kiss from God, caressed my face. In the days before my life had changed so dramatically, the Lord kept repeating in my spirit, "You are mine." On this day months later, he compassionately sealed his Isaiah 43 covenant with me, with a kiss.

Katherine Lawson

A Writer's Peace

Twenty-five years ago my life was turned upside down. My daughter and her husband were brutally murdered in their home, leaving my sweet, three year old granddaughter all alone. It was a long lonely journey, but I found comfort in the arms of my heavenly Father. He walked with me, he talked to me, and he literally carried me. God gave me a scripture that be- came my bread, Philippians 4:8 KJV, "whatsoever things are true, whatsoever things are honest, whatsoever things are just, whatsoever things are pure, whatsoever things are lovely, whatsoever things are of good report; if there be any virtue, and if there be any praise, think on these things." When the pain would get unbearable, I would hear that small voice saying, "I told you what to think on." I would heed to his voice and always triumph over my pain, all because of God's sweet love for me. It was a journey, but we as children of the Holy One are victorious through him. It was never promised that we would not experience sad- ness, loneliness, trials, and pain, but what my Father did promise is that he would not leave or forsake us. I am thrilled to have a relationship with such a lovely Father.

Bettie Mister

Problems Are Solved In Writing

As a young woman and even more so now that I'm much older, I have found when I go into my secret place to be with the Lord, I pick up my pen and write. My addressee is the Lord. It is here where the matters of my life are presented. I write, I write, I write. I make my case before the throne of my Father. One by one, I outline the situations, the stresses, and the problems that are pressing on my heart. The Holy Scripture says, "surely goodness and mercy shall fol- low me all the days of my life." As I deliver these mat- ters before my Father, he graciously takes them. I know that an answer will return with the stamp of his love, mercy, and guidance. His daughter has peti- tioned him and he has answered. Angels are dis- persed at his command. I am confident and know all is well. Yes, when I write to my Lord, my problems are solved.

Blondell Evans Phillips

I Obeyed And They Paid

It was time to meet the attorney. My sister's lawyer warned us he would be rude and downright mean. Praying ahead of time, the Holy Spirit gave instructions, "When you enter the room; touch the doorknob going in, going out, and coming back in. Once inside, touch that chair." Lord, that's not the likely chair of choice; are you sure? I thought, but out of obedience I followed directions. What would happen? I had no idea but I obeyed. As we waited, I could see angels lining the walls and I knew God was with us. The attorney knocked and turned the knob. "Hello Melissa, let's get right to it." He began to close the door with the inside of the knob now in hand. My sister spoke up sweetly and said, "I'm sorry but do you mean Michele?" He had gotten her name wrong so he said; "let me start this over." He walked back out of the room, re-closed the door, knocked, and twisted the knob coming back in. His attitude was completely different. That was enough to show the hand of God, but when he sat in the most awkward chair in the room and was the kindest man one could meet, we knew God had shifted the situation in her favor and he agreed with the demands of her lawyer. When you hear God's voice, no matter how "silly" the instructions may seem, trust him and trust the process. It's all working for your good.

LaTasha Sherrer

WORDS OF LIFE
(Life Prophetic Words)

The understanding of the life-word that God has given to me, is unity. The body of Christ has been subliminally separated from one another. Our mission is to unify. The mission of unity is to combat death. Death is now in disguise. The true definition of death is spiritual separation from God. Many of our brothers and sisters have been separated from fellowship with God (unaware) via compromise or from just the stress and strain of this evil atmosphere that we operate out of from day to day. I'm here to speak life over your lives and prophesy that you're being reconnected to Christ. I prophesy that your zeal to get intimate with the Father is reunited. I prophesy that the voice of the Holy Ghost will be heard clearly so that you might follow closely instructions in these dangerous times in which we now live.

C. L Simmons

I hear the Lord saying that everything that has come to bring death to your life; and everything that has come to flat line you, I speak a spiritual defibrillation to your spirit now, in the name of Jesus. I command everything to be resurrected to life. I decree and declare that you shall live and not die.

Deborah Simmons

ONE MAN FOR THE OTHER

It was January 12, 1997 on the dance floor of a night-club that I met a man name Lionel J. Traylor, who went by the nickname Suave. That night, my entire life changed.

I was on the dance floor dancing when he approached me and asked if he could have a dance. When the night finally ended, I was too prideful to ask him for his number, but to my surprise he didn't hesitate to ask me for mine. I eagerly pulled out a pen and wrote my number on a napkin giving it to him wondering when he would call. It was nearly three months later that I received a call from him. He began to tell me he was a backslider who wanted to rededi-cate his life to God and that he had started attending church again.

One day, I decided to find the church he was at-tending. Upon finding the address, I convinced my-self to attend a Wednesday night service. Opening the church doors was the hardest part for me because this was going to be my first time stepping into a church house as an adult. As I look back seeing myself sitting in church hearing the preacher's sermon on the grace of God it made me want to give my life to God. I met a man, who led me to a man named Jesus.

LaShawn Traylor

CHAPTER FIVE

LAUGHING ALL
THE WAY

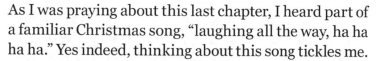

As I was praying about this last chapter, I heard part of a familiar Christmas song, "laughing all the way, ha ha ha ha." Yes indeed, thinking about this song tickles me.

I want to emphasize, again, that I will never laugh at your pain because I surely didn't laugh at mine. Hopefully, the word 'anecdote' will give you another way of thinking as you are coming out of where you are. In my study of laugher, I found Jewish jokes or anecdotes were used for wisdom and enlightenment, maybe not at the onset of the problem, but at some point, they were able to tell what they had been through with laughter. Also their comedy, humor, tragedy are intertwined and they spoke of their weak- ness and shortcomings. As you are grabbing hold to his Word, you may even laugh at yourself as you are telling about what you have been through.

Have you ever heard the cliché "Laughing all the way to the bank?" This saying denotes a person who is celebrating a financial victory, likely at the expense of others (usually, that kind of laughing is not a good thing, unless it's at the Devil).

I pray that after reading the writings of many of the contributors, seeing how they found humor in their situations, and (as some have explained) how reading or writing took them from problems to solutions. Even though the situation looks bad, through Christ Jesus the outcome doesn't have to be. The lord will not only bring you out, but will bring you out with joy and laughter. We can laugh all the way to the bank at expense of the enemy's destruction. He has to pay seven times. Keep in mind that the wealth of the wicked is laid up for the just. So, off to the bank we go—laughing all the way.

Let's use the Biblical accounts of a few individuals as examples. Job was a rich man who suffered great personal losses, yet his devotion toward God stayed strong. Abraham was a man that wanted a son more than anything. He had gotten very old and had not yet received his son, yet his devotion stayed strong.

The Apostle Paul suffered severe oppression from his enemies, yet he never lost his devotion to God. Stay with me; I have a point I'm trying to make.

You are going to find in life that some things come easier than others do. The key to the hard things is devotion. You may ask, "What does devotion have to do with laughter." A devoted person finds joy and laughter in the longest journeys of life. Have you ever driven a long distance with family and friends with you? You know it's going to be a very long ride so you bring along music that is full of energy, you may start out very early in the morning before dawn knowing that you will get a burst of energy at sunrise. You probably plan to make several stops at places to eat. At some point, you will switch drivers, so that you won't get too tired and everyone will stay safe. Then, the riders will take a nap while the driver drives. The fellowship will consist of the telling of jokes and stories and even visions of what it will be like when you all get to the destination. On the trip, everyone is as committed to getting to the end point as they are to enjoying the ride.

My question to you is, "Are you enjoying the ride or are you complaining and being spiteful toward God?" Are your clouds empty or are they full of devotion toward God. Do you enjoy your prayer life?

You know, I personally have gotten to the point that I absolutely love to pray. I can spend hours be- fore the Lord. I find a comfortable prayer space that brings me a lot of peace. I pray in bed. I pray kneeling beside the bed. I even pray in the car. I love it. Prayer gives me confidence and boldness. It gives me a sense of security. It reminds me that God is with me and that I can trust him. I like spending time with him because he is my closest and dearest friend.

Do you like to be a blessing to others? In case you didn't know, God is a spirit so you can't go to the store and buy him a gift and just give it to him. You have to give those gifts to other people. That is how we give to God. To the good-spirited person, there is no greater joy than being a blessing to other people. It's the most wonderful feeling. It resonates with us in a way that makes us feel like our journey here on Earth is worth- while.

We've done a lot of talking about laughter in this book, but I didn't want to end it without encouraging you to enjoy the trip. There is only one way to do it sincerely and that is by staying devoted to the things of God. Be happy as you read your Bible. Be joyful as you continue to be faithful in your church attendance. Make helping others something that you prioritize. I'm telling you that if you are serving the Lord with gladness, your clouds are filling up. God is not a man, but he is a person. He has feelings. He wants your love and devotion. He has angels on assignment to bless you. He will not withhold any good thing from you because you walk upright before him. When he finally releases that thing we almost felt would never come, we're going to be laughing all the way to the bank. He is going to do it. Just keep laughing and smiling. Let him drive if you get tired. Make a few pit stops along the way; enjoy life while you wait, and enjoy the most amazing journey ever.

There will be times when we have to 'take life on the chin.' It may hurt, but God is still good. Our journey is not a vacation. Vacations are a means by which we escape responsibility. Think of your life as a job you love. Think of it as something you would do even if there were no pay. Love what you do, but more importantly love the one you're doing it for. That person is Jesus. As you repeat the following prayer, I pray that your heart will be even more devoted to God as his purpose for your life, and that as you live your life you will be truly laughing all the way.

PRAYER

Lord Jesus,

I humbly reverence your name—for your name is far above every name. I want to thank you for all you have given me. I want to take this time especially to thank you for putting laughter in my soul. I am overjoyed because you have given me what I could not have given myself, salvation.

Lord, I know the world is filled with perilous situations, but you are with us to bring us comfort and peace. Right now, you are laughing at our enemies, so I know I have the victory. I'm laughing right along with you. Oh Lord laugh them to scorn. Lift up my heart that I may prophesy an end to every negative situation in my life.

We say, "He who laughs last laughs best." I know you always have the last laugh. As I receive the Spirit of your joy, give me the strength to be more devoted to you.

I pray this in Jesus' name—amen!

CHAPTER SIX

NOW LET M.E. TELL YOU!!!

Manifested Elevations – **FAITH**
Manifested Endorsements – **FAVOR**

Yes, indeed! I am very excited, knowing you are still here with me—still reading! I count it a blessing to be a blessing through my writing. I'm just as thrilled to answer a question you are likely asking:

"How did we get to Chapter Six?!"

The truth of the matter is a revision to the original content was required. You see, in the first "edition," I asked different people to share their testimonies *(as mentioned in Chapter Four)*. Everything those contributors provided was truly appreciated. From the text, emails, and reviews, a great number of people were blessed, to say the least. Later, however, I heard from other people who said they wanted to learn more about **ME**, my life experiences, and my testimonies.

Isn't it just like God to confirm His will for our lives? It is up to us to *OBEY*.

Today is September 22, 2020. We are months into a global pandemic—COVID 19, aka "Coronavirus"—that has disrupted life as we know it. We are living through an era when having faith in our Great God is more crucial now than ever before in modern history. We are also living during a time when our measures of faith are being tested and tried.

At this point, some of us would even beg to differ with the Apostle Paul, as he encouraged us in 2 Corinthians 4:8-9:

"We are troubled on every side, yet not distressed; we are perplexed, but not in despair; persecuted, but not forsaken; cast down, but not destroyed."

Even now, amid the pain we have experienced during COVID, God is **STILL** God. He promises never to leave nor forsake us. God cannot lie. God **DOES NOT** lie. We can and must take Him at His word and know He will bring us through to the other side victorious. Yes, indeed!!!

Personally, I have never seen so much pain, disappointment, and death. Daily, the number of fatalities attributed to COVID-19 continues to rise. The losses have been insurmountable. I'm not talking about just the loss of life, but also jobs, savings, investments, and relationships. Statistics report an increase in divorces, domestic violence, child abuse, homelessness, mental health issues, and various other sicknesses and diseases. Sadly, there is a rise in Christians walking away from their relationship with God. With all the uncertainties we are facing—even as we trust in God—the feelings of stress, abandonment, separation anxiety, fear, anger, being overwhelmed, and more are so real. However, now is not the time to lose faith in Jehovah-Jireh, our Provider.

In the midst of it ALL, God continues to prove Himself to be faithful! There are countless testimonies from those who have been healed and survived COVID-19. Some have even received an increase in their finances, bought homes and cars, got married, and had babies. Others have accepted Christ as their personal Savior, and their lives have completely turned around for the better. People are praying more and getting answers.

See? It is not all doom and gloom! Has it been easy? Not at all. Let us give ALL glory to God for brand-new mercies daily. Even now, He is showing Himself ALMIGHTY! Today is a great day to be alive and put all our trust in Him. I am so thankful to be on this side of Heaven, even in this season. My faith has increased!

"The name of the Lord is a strong tower: the righteous runneth into it and is safe." (Proverbs 18:10, KJV)

It's Too Funny Not to Be God was written for such a time as this—a time when we need to understand all we can about God and His promises to us for unconditional love and unending protection. He has given us **JOY** to be our weapon and strength in times of trouble. I cannot repeat this enough:

If we do not understand how God operates, we would not understand when to celebrate our victories! When we do not know when and what to celebrate, we are less likely to share what He has done because of the unique way God works on our behalf. The Apostle Paul could not have made it any clearer when he told us what God does in 1 Corinthians 1:27:

*"But God has chosen the **foolish** things of the world to put to shame the wise, and God has chosen the weak things of the world to put to shame the things which are mighty"* (emphasis added).

Let us not miss out on God or our blessings by boxing Him in. Do not deny others the opportunity to overcome just because we will not testify or share our stories for God's glory.

I am convinced there is more to be said to build your **faith**.

There is more to be said to help you identify the **favor** of the Lord upon your life.

There is more to be said to help you out with your **discernment**.

Just what *IS* "discernment"? Well, I will tell you! First, allow me a moment to define the word according to the Oxford Dictionary:

Discernment: (noun) *1. The ability to judge people and things well and to understand. 2. [In Christian contexts] Perception in the absence of judgment to obtain spiritual guidance and understanding.*

I, of course, will briefly discuss the latter meaning.

In our walk with God, using our gift of discernment is crucial. Often, we respond to circumstances with raw emotion. Understanding what goes on in our lives using *spiritual discernment* gives us a deeper insight into what we are experiencing. Once revealed, we can then respond appropriately. God desires that we thrive, not just survive. Many times, when we are faced with life's challenges, we find ourselves doing the opposite—just trying to survive. It is imperative that we remain clear on God's purpose, and discernment affords us the privilege to see beyond the natural eye. Psalms 119:66 reads:

"Teach me good judgment and knowledge: for I have believed Thy [God's] commandments."

As the Holy Spirit speaks to us, and we walk in more wisdom, we can apply our good judgment and knowledge to situations with **joy** and **laughter**.

Often, we quote scriptures, famous quotes, and cliches without seeking to experience what we speak. The very end of Ephesians 3:19 (NIV) speaks my heart for all of us: *"...that ye might be filled with all the fullness of God."* I am prayerful that we will be filled with love, joy, peace, power, healing, faith, prosperity, health, wealth, wisdom, and so much more.

I pray as you continue to read about *"M.E."*—my **Manifested Elevations (ch.7)**—that your *faith* is built and restored. I pray as I share more about *"M.E."*—my **Manifested Endorsements(ch.8)**—that you become more aware of God's *favor* in your life. As we journey together through the remainder of this book, I pray your **discernment** of **JOY** and **LAUGHTER** will increase! Let **ME** tell you!

Before, during, and after the pandemic, I release Psalm 126:2-3 to be your portion, in Jesus' Name!

"Then was our mouth filled with laughter, and our tongue with singing: then said they among the heathen, 'The Lord hath done great things for them.' The Lord hath done great things for us; whereof, we are glad."

IT'S TOO FUNNY NOT TO BE GOD! LOL! Turn the page now.

Let's go and grow!!!

CHAPTER SEVEN

M.E.—
MANIFESTED
ELEVATION
– FAITH

Let **ME** tell you... Joy is oozing out of me as I write! My *faith* level has increased, as I have yet again entered a time of sharing with you. These last chapters have me just as excited as I have been since the beginning of this book! As a matter of fact, this entire literary journey has been one of *faith* within itself.

I remember like it was yesterday when the Lord said, *"Share your written conversation!"*

Of course, I asked him, *"What does that mean?"*

Now, in case you haven't picked up on it yet, I don't know any other way to be but transparent. So, when I was instructed to write a book, I thought He meant to do so just for me, which would have made more sense. I picked up a pen and paper and started writing. My emotions were all over the place—excited, anxious, and overwhelmed at the same time! LOL!

Along the way, every time I attempted to get help with editing, the Lord stopped me in my tracks and said, *"I want you to think and write as if you were sharing a testimony or having a conversation on the phone and took notes."* Not long after, I realized my writing style is, indeed, "conversational"!

So, I'm going to keep "talking" as you keep "listening," and the Lord will keep blessing us both.

****

In these uncertain times—whether it is due to the pandemic or challenges that often come with daily living—we must exercise the measure of **FAITH** that is given to each of us individually. The more we use our *faith*, the more it will grow.

Revelation 12:11 says, *"...they overcome him by the blood of the Lamb, and by the word of their testimony..."*

You can read my book until you're blue in the face, but until you really know for yourself that He is God alone and that there are no coincidences, that "strange way your blessing manifested" could just be God increasing your *faith*.

Hebrews 11:6 says, *"...without faith, it is impossible to please Him..."*

LET'S FLOW IN FAITH!!!

My prayer is that we experience a 'Manifested Elevation' from God regularly. You are likely asking, *"What is that?"* Give me a moment to explain.

Manifested is something that is visible, revealed, obvious, and tangible. We are able to display it, demonstrate it, show it off, showcase it, and even do a show-and-tell, which, for many, means telling of God's goodness...to ***TESTIFY!*** Even though we had ***faith*** before the manifestation, there is a lift, an ascent, a rise, and an automatic altitude shift once it comes. We are suddenly soaring 30,000 feet above where we were before the manifestation.

Elevation refers to whatever we're speaking about, and it doesn't matter if it was cooking, cleaning, exercising, designing, or whatever else. We must believe when God delivers the answers, we can always remember the basics and stand on His promises.

Our ***faith***, confidence, certainty, knowledge, courage, hope, and trust in the Lord is renewed daily. If you are struggling in any of those areas, cry out to Him, ***"Lord, increase my faith!"*** (Luke 17:5) Trust me: He will do it for you. God will show Himself strong in everything that seems to weigh you down spiritually, physically, mentally, emotionally, or financially—all for His glory. ***Faith*** is the firm foundation under everything in our lives that makes it worth living. It is our hand on that which we cannot see.

Moving forward, I desire to build your *faith* as we pray this Word of God:

"...that your faith might not rest in the wisdom of men, but in the power of God" (1 Corinthians 2:5).

Allow **ME** *(Manifested Elevation)* to share some of my personal stories that built my *faith*. To this day, I say, it's **"Too Funny *Not* To Be God"**!

Laughter is defined as "the act of making merry or the emotional state of being amused." Interestingly, something most of us may not associate with laughter is *faith*. Yep! *Faith!* The reason why is because in every case where *faith* is displayed, God always gets the last laugh!

Now, buckle up for a journey of *faith*-stirring stories of a few of the **biblical** heroes of *faith*!

ENOCH: There are many things that pass right over us because we put our *faith* and trust in God. By an act of *faith*, Enoch skipped death completely. *"They looked all over and couldn't find him because God had taken him"* (Genesis 5). Based on reliable testimony, we know that before he was taken, *"he pleased God."* It is impossible to please God apart from *faith*. Why is that? Because anyone who wants to approach God must believe that He exists *and* cares enough to respond to those who seek Him.

RAHAB: By an act of *faith*, Rahab—the Jericho harlot—welcomed spies into her home and escaped the destruction that came on those who refused to trust God.

ABRAHAM: By an act of *faith*, Abraham said yes to God's call to travel to an unknown land that would later become his home. When he left on his journey, he had no idea where he was going, but he went, nonetheless. He lived as a stranger in the country promised to him, all while camping in tents. He kept his eyes set on an unseen city with real, eternal foundations—a city designed and built by God. Isaac and Jacob did the same while living under the same promise. By *faith*, Abraham's barren wife, Sarah, became pregnant at an old age, all because she believed the One who made a promise would do just what He said. Think about it: From one man's dead and shriveled loins, there are now people numbering into the millions!

NOAH: By an act of *faith*, Noah built a ship in the middle of dry land. He was warned about something he could not see and acted on what he was told. The result? His family was saved! His act of *faith* drew a sharp line between the evil of the unbelieving world and the rightness of the believing world. Noah was the good guy. He warned the people that a flood was coming, but they laughed at and mocked him. Rather than heed his warning, their wickedness became even more evident when they rejected the call of salvation. *"Get in the ship,"* Noah called to them. *"God wants to save you."* Imagine how the people bellowed in roaring laughter and said, *You crazy, old fool! You are delusional! You don't know what you are talking about!"* They had a good time laughing—at Noah's expense. Noah was probably saddened a bit about how he was rejected, but he kept moving and building. When he was done, he loaded the animals two by two, and his family and he prepared all that would be needed to sustain them for what was to come. *"Last call! Last call! I'm pleading with you to please turn from your evil ways and come into the ship. The Lord is about to send the rain. Hurry! Get on board!"* By then, I can imagine the people rolling around on the ground and holding their bellies as they laughed with hysterics. The Bible calls Noah "a preacher of righteousness." He perceived the evil of this world and let **ME** tell you something: *It was no laughing matter.*

I could go on and on, as there are so many more! Gideon. Barak. Samson. Jephthah. David. Samuel. The Prophets... By acts of *faith*, they toppled kingdoms, made justice work, and took the promises of God for themselves. They were protected from lions, fires, and sword thrusts, and turned disadvantages to advantages, won battles, and routed alien armies. There were also those who, under torture, refused to give in and be set free because they preferred something better: resurrection. I pray your *faith* has been *elevated!*

"...we walk by faith and not by sight" (2 Corinthians 5:7).

No matter how big the situation or concern, take it to the Lord. In all ways, acknowledge Him, and He shall direct your path. As we take God at His word and mix it with our *faith*, manifestations will come to pass—although they may not come when we want them. During the wait, we are not to become weary in our well-doing. We should continue to celebrate in advance! It pleases God when we trust Him, even when we feel our *faith* failing.

When I read and hear of good *faith* stories, such as the biblical accounts of the heroes of faith, I am full of hope and joy. I am further encouraged by the testimonies and victories we share amongst one another. There have been many tight spots in my life—hard times when I could not see a way out. Then, God stepped in! As I mentioned, God lovingly showed Himself strong. I didn't know whether to laugh, cry, or shout. Most of the time, I did all three and more! LOL!

Let **ME** share with you a couple of personal faith testimonies of when God showed up with *JOY* and *LAUGHTER*. It amazes me how God comes through for me time and again. The thankfulness, gratitude, and joy in my heart are indescribable! I used to ask myself, *"Is this real?"* Well, God is real, and His ways are past our understanding. It seems the more I tell of His goodness, the more unprecedented and unexplained blessings show up.

So, keep reading...keep "listening"! I'm just getting started and believe my stories will bless you as I demonstrate why I continue to say that it's **"Too Funny *Not* To Be God"**!

Shower of JOY

One of my very first friends was Kim. Our friendship dated back to the age of five. Even though we were so young, we had great times. Kim and I were a lot like sisters. We would laugh, play, run, cry, and profess we would be "together forever."

Well, as life would have it, we lost contact for over ten years but were able to reconnect right before I got married. Not long after, however, we lost touch again. It wasn't intentional; it was just "life." That time, it bothered me because I believed we both wanted to be in each other's life. I began to pray and intentional prayer about finding Kim. I realized I had to believe God, even for something as "small" as that.

One Saturday, I was either talking to my friend, Kitty, or I was with her (I cannot clearly recall...I'm telling my age here. LOL!). While with her, she told me about a baby shower she was going to with her friend, Connie. For whatever reason, she then asked me to come with her and assured me it would be okay.

Will somebody **PLEASE** tell me why in the **WORLD** I would go to a baby shower of someone I did not know? All I knew was that it was Connie's sister-in-law.

Okay. I'll admit it. I went. LOL!

On the way, I stopped and bought a gift. While at the baby shower, observing the people mixing and mingling was a pleasant experience. When it was time to settle down for the mom-to-be to open her gifts, it was then I finally had the chance to see the person the party was for.

IT WAS MY LONG, LOST FRIEND! KIM!!!

It was, for sure, a Kodak moment. We hugged. We kissed. We cried. We hugged. We kissed. We cried. (You see where I'm going with this, right?) Eventually, we settled down and let the baby shower resume. I know our "chance" reunion was nobody but God. The *JOY* we experienced was insurmountable!

FAITH FOR FUN STUFF – DISNEY

Being blessed with four very grateful children, for them, trips to Jackson, Tennessee, or Hot Springs, Arkansas, were good enough. As for me, I desired to take them to Disneyland one day. Not too many months later, I was blessed with free tickets for the whole family!

Now, it took *faith* to believe God for where we were going to stay and how we would eat while there. I knew it was part of God's blueprint, so I moved forward with planning for the trip. Admittedly, there were times when doubt tried to set in, but I remembered I had asked the Lord specifically for the family trip. My confidence soon rose to the top. I had nothing but high expectations about what God was getting ready to do for me!

I worked at FedEx at the time, so the flights and lodging were discounted. Wait. Do you think I'm writing about the family vacation? I'm not. I'm sharing how we can all believe in God, even for the **smallest** things.

Let's fast-forward...

A new ride called 'Jurassic Park' had just opened, and it was the first one we went on once in the park. The ride was exhilarating! However, when it ended, some of the people exiting with us were talking loudly and walking fast. I sensed something was wrong, but what could it have been? I was clueless.

I had to go to Guest Services for something and, once there, noticed how crowded it was. I also observed employees passing out forms to many in the room. One was placed in my hands, and I asked, *"Why?"*

The manager asked, *"Were you just on Jurassic Park?"*

"Yes."

He then apologized for the inconvenience and explained there was a malfunction that caused oil to splash on some of the riders.

"...the truth shall make you free" (John 8:32).

I told the manager my family was not affected by the oil and that we had no oil on us at all. He looked at me with amazement as I spoke the **truth**. He then made a special note on my form and asked me to complete it anyway.

That day, the park gave me $150.00 in Disney Bucks!!! That wasn't it, though. Later, I received a check in the mail and VIP tickets for the entire family for Disney World in Florida! Look at God! I would love to tell you all about the VIP treatment that included no waiting in lines, but perhaps that's for another day... another book. Rest assured of this: It was amazing!

I wish I had more time to share with you, but we must move on to the next chapter.

In closing, I encourage you to always put your *faith* muscle to work—from the least to the greatest!

CHAPTER EIGHT

M.E.—MANIFEST ENDORSEMENT — <u>FAVOR</u>

"May the favor of the Lord our God rest on us; establish the work of our hands for us—yes, establish the work of our hands" (Psalm 90:17).

Again, let **ME** tell you! Just reading the words of that scripture brings life and joy to my soul!

Let's stir up the manifestations as we ***"flow with favor"***! The blessings of the Lord rest upon each of us. We must admit, however, that there are times when the Lord blesses us, ***favors*** us, and graces us that it doesn't seem real. If it doesn't seem to be real, we may sometimes feel as though we are undeserving. When we experience the Lord's *favor*, there should be a new level of confidence, knowing we received approval straight from Heaven. God's **endorsement** means everything!

As you continue walking in faith, trust in God's plan for you. That which you have prayed for will come to pass. Not only will the Lord release your blessing, but He will also cause everything connected to your release to come in alignment with His Word. Don't give up on His promises for you, for nothing is impossible with God. Even when it seems like manifestation is "taking forever," know that with His perfect wisdom and timing, just **ONE** word from Him will turn it around in your *favor*.

You might be wondering, *"Why is that concept important to know and embrace?"* (I love trying to anticipate and answer the questions that may be floating around in your head! LOL!)

Well, one reason is this: If we do not know how God works in our lives, we may miss Him!

"When we don't understand our testimonies, we won't understand our victories!" ~ Brenda Ferguson ~ (Yes, indeed! I approve this message amid the 2020 Presidential Election!)

"...houses filled with all kinds of good things you did not provide, wells you did not dig, and vineyards and olive groves you did not plant—then when you eat and are satisfied..." (Deuteronomy 6:11, NIV).

What a powerful word of *favor* and covenant! There are places we work and live, schools we attend, cars we drive, events we go to, and even some of the places where we eat that are **ALL** God's hand of *favor*. It's time to wake up and see all that He is doing for us, no matter how small it seems. His *favor* counts us in where men would count us out. The things we have that we know we didn't qualify for should stir continuous praise for God's mind-boggling *favor*! The more we are aware of His *favor*, the more we should see just how blessed and victorious we truly are.

It is God who moves in the hearts of those connected to your blessings. That "one person" may be in a position to make a final decision regarding the blessing for which you prayed. Whether they know it or not, they are cooperating with what God has already **endorsed** for your life. **(My God! I felt that!!!)** When God's hand of *favor* manifests in your life, think of it as God looking past everyone else and choosing **you**. Now, that's **"Too Funny Not To Be God"**!

Sometimes, I think my name should have been Brenda *"Faith"* or Brenda *"Favor"* instead of Brenda *"Faye."* (That is said in complete humility, coupled with gratefulness.) When I look back over my life, I think of the lyrics that say, ***"When I think of the goodness of Jesus and all He has done for me, my soul cries out, 'Hallelujah'! Thank You, God, for saving me!"*** I am so thankful to have access to His Word. One of my favorite scriptures is found in Proverbs 3:5-6:

"Trust in the Lord with all your heart and lean not on your own understanding; in all your ways, acknowledge Him, and He shall direct your paths."

I depend on those verses to remind me to trust in Him with **everything** I have, not to lean on my own understanding, and to talk to Him before making all decisions. No matter what plan is set before me, I pray, *"Lord, lead me, guide me, and direct me."* My greatest victories have come from submitting my plans to His will. When the doors burst wide open, that's God's *favor*!

Let **ME** tell you! Again, I want to share a couple of my *"favor flow"* testimonies that are sure to bless you and bring you to **laughter**.

The Airlines

Having worked for FedEx for over 23 years, I've traveled extensively—both business and personal. There are countless stories I can tell about my travels, including tales about my luggage, being moved up in lines, having my seating changed (after being told there were no seats available), free tickets, miles added to my accounts, and so much more.

At this time, however, I want to stir up your memory about things that have happened to **YOU** so that we can **ALL** shout together, *"Lord, thank You for Your favor!"*

Early the morning of October 5, 2020, my daughter and her husband notified me that their baby was on the way. I planned to drive out that following week, but at 2:00 a.m., I found myself praying and packing. I told the Lord I wanted to arrive at the hospital before my grandson came. Even though this was my daughter's first delivery (the first *typically* takes longer than others), I didn't feel comfortable thinking I would make it to the hospital in time. I knew it would take me seven hours to drive there, and the tickets were too expensive to purchase that same day, so I prayed a fervent prayer: *"Lord, I need your help. I trust You to make this happen."*

Trust in the Lord was in full effect!

I felt pressed to call the airport again at around 4:00 a.m. It was then I learned the flight I needed to take was leaving Dallas around 7:00 a.m. The agent I spoke to asked, *"What's your frequent flyer mileage?"* Admittedly, I was probably too excited and nervous during the first call to even think about that. Needless to say, I was able to get a ticket with the number of miles previously flown. I honestly believe most were just put on there that morning—and no one can tell me differently. LOL! It is my belief today that Heaven opened American Airlines to **endorse** me. I only paid $83.00 for a roundtrip ticket!!!

That's not quite the end of the story, though...

I didn't like my seat on the flight but was willing to take anything. I didn't utter a word to the attendants because I was simply thankful to be on that plane.

Meanwhile, I noticed one of the flight attendants kept smiling at me a little "extra." When she had the chance, she said I looked familiar (although I didn't know her whatsoever). The next thing I knew, I was being escorted to First Class! She quickly shared with me that she knew my son and followed his ministry. That day, I flew in my *favor* **AND** my son's *favor*!

Did I make it to the hospital in time? **YES**, with time to spare! I was able to visit with my daughter Liz and son-in-love Mike, before my grandson,

Miloh Amir was born!!!

I have so many stories of *favor*. It's hard to choose, but let me share another quick one...

A Car from a Call

Those who know me will tell you I have **NO** problem striking up a conversation with a stranger. Many times, I am certain I have entertained an angel unaware!

A friend of mine told a lady I could help her out with a business matter. I didn't know the lady who was referred to me, but I knew my expertise could be beneficial. Once I received the woman's call, we ended with her seemingly very pleased with my service.

Quick sidebar: Keep the following in mind—I had talked to the Lord about getting another car, but that had nothing to do with the call.

Let me demonstrate to you how intentional God is...

Almost a week later, I received a call on my home phone. On the other end was the same lady! (It was unusual because our business took place over my **cell** phone.) During our conversation, she told me the help I provided had been a tremendous blessing to her business financially. **Well, praise God!** She had already thanked me for my services (which were given free of charge), but during that second call, she kept said, *"You just don't know what that did for me!"* When she then asked, *"Is there anything I can do for you?"* the farthest thing from my mind was telling her I needed a car. (If she had told me she was a car dealer, I might have thought differently). After allowing that question to slip through a couple more times, she pressed in on me—hard. It was then I told her, *"I need a car."*

Mind you: I was **laughing** as I said it because I did not know God's *favor* was actually posed in the woman's persistent question.

Much to my surprise, the tone of her voice never

changed when she said, *"Okay. Let me make a few phone calls."* The very next day, she called me back and asked, *"Can you get from Memphis, Tennessee to Ennis, Texas? My friend has a car ready and waiting for you."*

By faith, I told her, *"Yes, I will be there."*

Now, **this** is what I've been trying to tell you about the *favor* of God! Not only does it not seem fair at times, but it can also seem really strange. LOL! Because I understand how God works, I knew it was ***"Too Funny* (again) *Not To Be God"***! It was nobody but Him!

I am here to testify that my Godmom and two awesome brothers from my church drove me to Texas to pick up my **BRAND-NEW CAR!** When I told the woman yes, I had *NO* clue it was a **BRAND-NEW** Ford Focus with woodgrain—and leather seats (to me, it looked like a baby Mercedes Benz)! No downpayment was necessary, and, with *discounts*, my monthly payment was only $196.00!

Let **ME** tell you! I am so thankful the same *favor* still rests upon my life today!

CHAPTER NINE

A *JOY* THAT REMAINS

"So, David inquired of the Lord, saying, 'Shall I pursue this troop? Shall I overtake them?' And He answered him, 'Pursue, for you shall surely overtake them and, without fail, recover all" (1 Samuel 30:8).

God knew everything we would need to live victoriously while on this earth. In John 14:18, Jesus said, *"I will not leave you comfortless,"* so He left the Holy Spirit to live on the inside of us. Not only does the Holy Spirit give us power and peace, but He also gives us fruits for our daily walk.

God is sovereign. The days we are experiencing, He saw before the beginning of time. Even now, He is with us and giving us the strategies needed to win the war. However, it is up to us to pick up our weapons and fight the good fight of faith—and not be weary in well-doing. Nothing happening in our lives catches God by surprise.

"We are troubled on every side, yet not distressed; we are perplexed, but not in despair; persecuted, but not forsaken; cast down, but not destroyed" (2 Corinthians 4:8).

Let me encourage you right now to "get up from where you are." No, it may not be easy because it appears you are surrounded by every negative thing under the sun, but I am here to remind you of this one amazing truth:

You are surrounded by Christ, His blood, and a host of war angels fighting on your behalf! The Lord is your strength today and always!

Heartaches, despair, depression, anxiety, suicide, murder, domestic violence, cancer, and all manners of sickness and disease (COVID-19 included) are not greater than the power of **JESUS'** name! Call on Him!

There are days I struggle just to keep moving. I then call upon the name of the Lord, play some praise and worship music, sing along, and pray aloud. Although the CDC recommends that we wear masks during the pandemic, I implore you to remove your mask *spiritually* by not allowing the enemy to close your mouth and stop you from worshipping our Lord with your highest praise.

God says in His Word that He wants our ***JOY to REMAIN*** and that our ***JOY be FULL***! That tells me even in hard times and during the most challenging circumstances we face, we will not be destroyed by the enemy. Sometimes, that may require us to push ourselves like never before. God cannot lie. He gives us **JOY** for our ashes, turns our mourning into dancing, and promises to prosper us in the midst of a famine! It's time to rise, for He has sent us **JOY** amid our turmoil.

Even if you are reading this book in 2022 (or later), God's Word still stands. He will always do just what He says. Read His Word aloud...***often***. Never throw in the towel on what God can do because He loves you with an everlasting love. No matter how bad "life" gets, He will make sure you always know He is **right there** with you. You won't "just exist"; you will go through and arrive on the other side with ***JOY***!

Before I go, just know I could have written and broken down every word in Greek and Hebrew, but I had to obey what God said to do regarding this project. He instructed me to "have a conversation," and I am assured this book has blessed, encouraged, and empowered somebody.

In closing, I leave you with these words:

You **WILL** overtake the enemy! You **WILL** recover it ***ALL***! Reclaim your **JOY** today!

"These things have I spoken unto you, that My joy might remain in you, and that your joy might be full" (St. John 15:11, KJV).

AFTERWORD

Sometimes after reading, I wonder to myself if I have gotten all that the author intended for me to get.

My prayer for each of you is that after you finish reading this book, or even the introduction, that you experience and receive the words of Jesus in the following scripture:

These things I have spoken to you, that my joy may remain in you, and that your joy may be full.

—John 15:11 NKJV

Always remember that the joy you have is the strength you need in every situation. And, when your joy is full, your laughter rises up as your weapon.

CONTRIBUTORS
(Alphabetical order by last name)

Allen, Angie
   "Court to Courtship" (p. 48)
      Angie Allen
      Memphis, TN

Barnes, J. E.
   "The Write to Exhale" (p. 49)
      Rev. J. E. Barnes, M. Div., M.A.
      Memphis, TN

Becton, Stephanie Y.
   "From Hole to Held" (p. 50)
   Life Church
   Cordova, TN

Burks, Addie
      "All in One Call" (p. 42)
      Attorney Addie Burks
      Memphis, TN

Byers, Michaele
      "It's Too Funny Not To Be God"(p. 40)
      Minister Michaele Byers
      Faith Christian Church

Carter, Salina A.
    "Reading Brings Life" (p. 51)
    Salina A. Carter RN
    Solomon's Porch, Atlanta, GA

Ducker, Paris
    "What Shall I Do?" (p. 52)
    Paris Ducker
    www.Chaos2Clarity.org

Fran, Lady
    "The Blessing in Writing" (p. 54)
    Lady Fran
    West Bloomfield, MI

Gesing, Bob
Gesing, Cheryl
    "How to Get Stoned at a Camp Meeting" (p. 55)
    Bob and Cheryl Gesing
    Undiscovered Treasure Ministries

Givens, Diane
    "A Continuous Calm" (p. 56)
    Diane Givens
    Memphis, TN

Head, Lisa
    "Off the Shelf" (p. 57)
    Lisa Head, Intercessor
    LisaHead81@yahoo.com

Lawson, Katherine
        "The Kiss" (p. 58)
        Dr. Katherine Lawson, Executive Director
        Victims to Victory, Memphis, TN

Mister, Bettie
        "A Writer's Peace" (p. 59)
        Bettie Mister
        BettieMister@Comcast.net

Norwood, Diane
        "Laughter in a Relationship" (p. 41)
        Prophetess Diane Norwood
        Just for Christ Ministries, Millington, TN

Phillips, Blondell Evans
        "Problems are Solved in Writing" (p. 60)
        Minister Blondell Evans Phillips
        Memphis, TN

Self, Dell
        "The Orange Dress" (p. 61)
        Dell Self, *www.SpeakThroughMe.com*
        self-publishing service//faith-based speaking

Sherrer, LaTasha
        "I Obeyed and They Paid" (p. 63)
        LaTasha Sherrer
        Milwaukee, WI

Simmons, C. L.
Simmons, Deborah
> "Words of Life" (p. 64)
> Apostle C.L. Simmons/Pastor Deborah Simmons
> Rhema Life Deliverance Intl. Ministries

Traylor, LaShawn
> "One Man for the Other" (p. 65)
> LaShawn Traylor
> The Epicenter Church, Jackson, MS

ABOUT THE AUTHOR

Brenda Faye Ferguson serves the kingdom and the community with passion as she encourages, empowers, and places a mandate on others to experience the joy of the Lord through a right relationship with him and others. As she lives her life on purpose, she is of- ten found saying, "God is concerned about souls, and I am too!" Her love for her family and God's people is quite amazing as well as contagious. She shares in her day-to-day conversations, and in those select moments, "Pray that I stay in proper alignment" with God so that he will continue to talk to me that I may hear him and obey." For Brenda, hearing God for her- self, and prophetically for others, has been a joy; she is humbled that God has counted her worthy.

Brenda's licensing and ordination are accredited to her strong leadership skills, her heart of a servant coupled with a spirit of excellence to her pastor from her home church. Having numerous testimonies of supernatural experiences with the Lord in the areas of faith, prayer, prophetic, and altar work, has become who she is—her DNA and spiritual brand.

God has placed an anointing on her life that has opened doors of opportunity to lead prayers, speak, and train congregations as well as lead conferences, small groups, altar workers, new member groups, prophetic teams and more. Brenda is a vessel truly used by God.

Her passionate walk with the Lord brought identification and purpose in ministry. Creating Flow Ministries, Inc. was founded in 2007 to bring alignment, organization, and consultation to ministries and business owners around the world.

Even though Brenda has ministered with many renowned leaders in this nation and is very active on intercessory prayer teams, leadership development teams, prophetic teams, and strategic business teams, her personal and primary focus remains loving God, her family, and friends with joy and laughter.

Printed in the United States
by Baker & Taylor Publisher Services